Believing in Jesus

Loveland, Colorado

Group's R.E.A.L. Guarantee to you:

This Group resource incorporates our R.E.A.L. approach to ministry—one that encourages long-term retention and life transformation. It's ministry that's:

Relational
Because learner-to-learner interaction enhances learning and builds Christian friendships.

Experiential
Because what learners experience through discussion and action sticks with them up to 9 times longer than what they simply hear or read.

Applicable
Because the aim of Christian education is to equip learners to be both hearers and doers of God's Word.

Learner-based
Because learners understand and retain more when the learning process takes into consideration how they learn best.

SENIOR HIGH BIBLE STUDY SERIES

Believing in Jesus

Copyright © 2003 Group Publishing, Inc.

All rights reserved. No part of this book may be reproduced in any manner whatsoever without prior written permission from the publisher, except where noted in the text and in the case of brief quotations embodied in critical articles and reviews. For information write Permissions, Group Publishing, Inc., Dept. PD, P.O. Box 481, Loveland, CO 80539.

Visit our Web site: www.grouppublishing.com

Credits
Contributing Authors: Bob Buller and Dick Hardel
Editor: Kelli B. Trujillo
Creative Development Editor: Amy Simpson
Chief Creative Officer: Joani Schultz
Copy Editor: Linda Marcinkowski
Art Director: Sharon Anderson
Cover Art Director/Designer: Jeff A. Storm
Cover Photographer: Daniel Treat
Print Production Artist: Stephen Beer
Production Manager: DeAnne Lear

Unless otherwise noted, Scripture taken from the HOLY BIBLE, NEW INTERNATIONAL VERSION®. Copyright © 1973, 1978, 1984 by International Bible Society. Used by permission of Zondervan Publishing House. All rights reserved.

ISBN 0-7644-2476-9

10 9 8 7 6 5 4 3 2 1   12 11 10 09 08 07 06 05 04 03

Printed in the United States of America.

CONTENTS

Introduction **4**

STUDY 1 — **Shame on You** **7**
> **The Point:** Sin results in guilt and shame.
> **Scripture Source:** Genesis 3:1-24; John 8:1-11;
> Romans 3:23

STUDY 2 — **I Was Wrong** **17**
> **The Point:** To overcome sin, we must admit we're wrong.
> **Scripture Source:** 1 Samuel 13:2-14; Psalm 51:1-17;
> Jonah 3:1-10

STUDY 3 — **Sentenced to Death** **28**
> **The Point:** Through Jesus' death on the cross, we can receive forgiveness for our sins.
> **Scripture Source:** Psalm 22; Matthew 27:32-56; John 3:16

STUDY 4 — **He Is Risen Indeed!** **38**
> **The Point:** Through faith in Jesus, we can experience new life.
> **Scripture Source:** Matthew 28:1-20; Romans 10:9-11

Changed 4 Life **47**

about faith 4 life

BELIEVING IN JESUS

The tension is almost unbearable. The score is tied. The clock is counting down. Then, in the final few seconds of the championship game, it happens: The quarterback himself runs the ball into the end zone. The game is won! The crowd goes wild! Soon afterward, the interviews begin. "First of all, I'd like to thank my Lord and Savior Jesus Christ," the quarterback says.

Lots of people seem to talk about Jesus. Music, movie, and TV celebrities sometimes thank him when they win awards. Politicians talk about him on the campaign trail. And of course, plenty of regular people say his name a lot for, uh, *other* reasons.

Who exactly is Jesus? And what does it really mean to believe in him?

Who exactly *is* Jesus? And what does it really mean to believe in him? Does being a Christian mean going to church or doing good deeds? Or something more?

These four studies will help you guide your teenagers into a clear understanding of what it means to believe in Jesus. They'll be confronted with their need for Jesus' forgiveness and will encounter the true meaning of his death and resurrection.

In the first study, teenagers will learn that sin has serious consequences: guilt and shame. They'll look closely at the first sin in the Garden of Eden and will investigate how shame and guilt disrupt humanity's relationship with God. They'll be challenged to consider how they can experience freedom from the sin that plagues their own lives.

In the second study, students will discover that repentance is an essential element in restoring their relationship with God. Through hands-on activities, they'll experience the bondage of sin and the freedom of forgiveness. They'll examine biblical examples of repentance and will have an opportunity to personally repent of sins they struggle with.

Teenagers will step inside the story of Jesus' crucifixion in the third study. They'll explore what they might have felt if they had been present at Jesus' death, and they'll be impacted as they consider the pain Jesus endured for their sake. Students will look deeper into some very familiar Bible passages to discover that through Jesus' death, they can find true forgiveness for their sins.

End things with a bang during this final study that uses surprise to celebrate Jesus' resurrection. A party, art project, and short dramas all come together in this study to hammer home the truth that teenagers can experience new life through faith in Jesus. They'll wrap up their exploration of faith in Christ by considering Jesus' resurrection appearance to Mary and the Great Commission Jesus gave to the disciples in Galilee. Students will commit to live in resurrection joy throughout the year as they celebrate the forgiveness Jesus provides.

Faith 4 Life *Believing in Jesus* will help senior high students understand how they can have a restored relationship with God through faith in Christ. They'll live in forgiveness and grace as they take the challenge to live as disciples in joy and new life.

SENIOR HIGH BIBLE STUDY SERIES

Faith 4 Life: Senior High Bible Study Series helps teenagers take a Bible-based approach to faith and life issues. Each book in the series contains these important elements:

• Life application of Bible truth
Faith 4 Life studies help teenagers understand what the Bible says and then apply that truth to their lives.

• A relevant topic
Each Faith 4 Life book focuses on one main topic, with four studies to give your students a thorough understanding of how the Bible relates to that topic. These topics were chosen by youth leaders as the ones most relevant for senior high students.

• One point
Each study makes one point, centering on that one theme to make sure students really understand the important truth it conveys. This point is stated upfront and throughout the study.

• Simplicity
The studies are easy to use. Each contains a "Before the Study" box that outlines any advance preparation required. Each study also contains a "Study at a Glance" chart so you can quickly and easily see what supplies you'll need and what each study will involve.

• Action and interaction
Each study relies on experiential learning to help students learn what God's Word has to say. Teenagers discuss and debrief their experiences in large groups, small groups, and individual reflection.

• Reproducible handouts
Faith 4 Life books include reproducible handouts for students. No need for student books!

• Tips, tips, and more tips
Faith 4 Life studies are full of "FYI" tips for the teacher, providing extra ideas, insights into young people, and hints for making the studies go smoothly.

• Flexibility
Faith 4 Life studies include optional activities and bonus activities. Use a study as it's written, or use these options to create the study that works best for your group.

• Follow-up ideas
At the end of each book, you'll find a section called "Changed 4 Life." This section provides ideas for following up with your students to make sure the studies stick with them.

Use Faith 4 Life studies to show your teenagers how the Bible is relevant to their lives. Help them see that God can invade every area of their lives and change them in ways they can only imagine. Encourage your students to go deeper into faith—faith that will sustain them for life! Faith 4 Life, forever!

STUDY 1

SHAME ON YOU

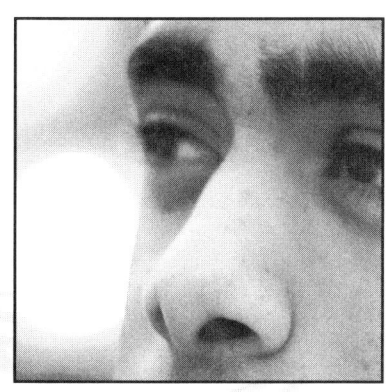

"Caught on Tape!"

There it is, just another lurid TV talk show whose hidden cameras caught people in the act. Maybe they were filmed lying, stealing, or cheating. And before they knew it, their actions were broadcast before a national television audience!

Would you want that to happen to you? *Probably not*.

The reality is that we've all been "caught on tape." God sees us when we sin—we can't hide from him no matter how hard we try—and that sin significantly affects our lives. It results in a weight of guilt and shame that distorts our self-image, disrupts our relationships with others, and destroys our intimacy with God.

In this study teenagers will explore the stories of some people who faced serious shame: the woman caught in adultery and publicly accused of her crime, and Adam and Eve who were "caught" by God after disobeying him in the Garden. They'll take a close look at their own lives and will consider the effects of their sin on their relationship with God.

THE POINT

Sin results in guilt and shame.

SCRIPTURE SOURCE

Genesis 3:1-24
This passage describes Adam and Eve's sin and their resulting feelings of guilt and shame.

John 8:1-11
John describes Jesus' encounter with a woman caught in adultery.

Romans 3:23
The writer explains that all people have sinned.

THE STUDY AT A GLANCE

#1 For Starters
10-15 Minutes

■ **I WISH I COULD FORGET!**

What students will do:
Share their most embarrassing moments with one another, determine whose was the worst, and discuss embarrassment and shame.

■ **OPTIONAL ACTIVITY**
10-15 Minutes

What students will do:
Play an embarrassing game then discuss embarrassment and shame.

SUPPLIES:
- "I Can't Believe I'm Doing This!" handouts (p. 15)

#2 Bible Truth
20-25 Minutes

■ **FIG LEAVES AND STONES**

What students will do:
Discuss the first sin and its effects on God's relationship with humanity.

SUPPLIES:
- Bibles
- "Sin's Beginnings" handouts (p. 16)
- pens or pencils
- dry-erase marker
- full-length mirror

#3 Life Application
15-20 Minutes

■ **A LOOK IN THE MIRROR**

What students will do:
Consider the effects of their own sin and thank Jesus that he can free them from shame and guilt.

SUPPLIES:
- Bibles
- full-length mirror
- rag

8 FAITH 4 LIFE

BEFORE THE STUDY

Before the study, if you choose to do the Optional Activity, make several photocopies of the "I Can't Believe I'm Doing This!" handout (p. 15). You'll need approximately one copy for every ten students. Cut the cards apart and gather the exact number of cards you'll need, based on the number of participants. Make sure that you have at least two of each type of card. (If you have less than ten students, narrow down your pile to only two or three types of instruction cards. Make additional copies of the handout so that you can gather the correct number of cards bearing the instructions you selected.) Fold all the cards in half, mix them up, and set them aside.

For the Bible Truth section, you'll need to make one photocopy of the "Sin's Beginnings" handout (p. 16) for every two participants. You'll also need to bring a full-length mirror and a dry-erase marker. If you have a large group (bigger than twenty) you'll need to bring several full-length mirrors and additional dry-erase markers. Bring at least one cloth rag for the Life Application activity.

Use all four Bible studies in this book in sequential order to help your students understand what it truly means to make a faith commitment to Jesus.

If your group is larger than twenty, have teenagers form groups of four to eight to share their embarrassing stories, and make sharing a story optional. When representatives from each group share their stories with the whole class, set a time limit that forces them to tell the story quickly. This way you can save some time *and* laugh together as the volunteers tell their stories at the speed of light.

FOR STARTERS

10 to 15 minutes

I WISH I COULD FORGET!

Say: **We've all had them. They make our hearts race. They make our blood pressure rise. They make us want to run for cover. We cringe at the very thought of them. They're our most embarrassing moments. Right now, think of your own most embarrassing moment.**

After about thirty seconds, invite teenagers to form trios and each take about one minute to quickly share their most embarrassing moment with their group members. Tell trios that after they've heard each person's story, their job is to decide together which story was the most embarrassing.

When trios have narrowed down their selections, invite a representative from each group to stand in front and share with the rest of the students the most embarrassing moment his or her trio selected. Explain that students will vote on all of the stories and will pick the most embarrassing one of the entire group, so encourage the storytellers to be as dramatic and humorous as possible!

Once all the stories have been told, **say:**

> **Think for a moment about all the stories you heard. Which is the most embarrassing? Decide which one you'd like to vote for—but you can't vote for the story from your own trio. You'll vote by cheering, so make sure you cheer for every story, but cheer the very loudest for the story you think is the most embarrassing.**

Briefly mention each story and allow time for cheering after each one. Determine which story got the loudest cheers, and declare that story the winner.

Say: **These stories were all pretty embarrassing! I certainly wouldn't want them to happen to me! It probably wasn't easy for all of you to share your stories because you wish you could forget they ever happened. And you probably each have some stories that you *didn't* share with your group. They were just too embarrassing. In fact, they may even make you feel ashamed.**

Have students return to their trios and **ask:**

- **What's the difference between feeling embarrassed and feeling ashamed?**
- **What causes embarrassment?**
- **What causes shame?**
- **If I had asked you to share your most shameful moment instead of just your most embarrassing one, would you have wanted to do it? Why or why not?**

Say: **We all face times of embarrassment in our lives, and we also all deal with feelings of shame. Often those feelings are caused by something we've done, something we know isn't right.** Sin results in guilt and shame. **Sin affects the way we view ourselves, the way we relate to others, and most importantly, the way we relate to God.**

As a survivor of the teenage years, inevitably you've had a few embarrassing doozies of your own! Share an *appropriate* embarrassing moment from your life. It will be sure to get students laughing and will also help them see that you can relate to what they're going through as adolescents!

OPTIONAL ACTIVITY

10 to 15 minutes

Instead of the "I Wish I Could Forget!" activity, get discussion started by having teenagers play this game.

Select a large playing area such as a gymnasium, large room, or an open space outdoors. Give each teenager a folded card from the "I Can't Believe I'm Doing This!" handout (p. 15), but instruct them not to open their cards yet.

Say: Each of you has been handed some directions for an action you're supposed to do. When I say "Go!" your job is to unfold your card, read your instructions, and then immediately begin doing exactly what your card says. There is at least one other person in our group who has received the same directions, so you need to wander around the playing area following your instructions until you're able to find all of the people who are doing the same thing. Once you find them, stick together, but don't stop following your directions until I've asked you to stop.

Ask teenagers if they have any questions. When everyone is ready to play the game, direct teenagers to spread out around the room, then **say: Go!**

Once everyone has found their group members, or after five minutes have passed, tell students they can stop acting out the instructions on their cards. Invite them to **discuss** these questions with the other members of their groups:

- **How did you feel when you first read your instructions? How did you feel when you started doing what they said?**
- **What was funny about this activity? What was embarrassing?**
- **What are some other situations from your life in which you've felt embarrassed?**
- **What's the difference between feeling embarrassment and feeling shame?**
- **What causes embarrassment?**
- **What causes shame?**

Say: We all face times of embarrassment in our everyday lives, and we also all deal with feelings of shame. We try to hide the things we're ashamed about—we try to keep them in the dark. Often shame is caused by something we've done, something we know isn't right. Sin results in guilt and shame. Sin affects the way we view ourselves, the way we relate to others, and most importantly, it affects the way we relate to God.

BIBLE TRUTH

20 to 25 minutes

FIG LEAVES AND STONES

Have students stay in their trios from the first activity. Give each trio a copy of the "Sin's Beginnings" handout (p. 16) and invite them to take up to ten minutes to read the Bible passage, discuss the questions, and create their lists.

Prompt teenagers to gather back together as a large group, and ask trios to share their thoughts from the first two questions on the handout. Then **say:**

> I think we can all relate to how Adam and Eve felt. We've all had moments where we wanted to hide something we'd done. Perhaps we were able to hide it from our parents, a friend, or a teacher, but we're *never* able to hide our sins from God.

Prop the full-length mirror up in front of the group, and ask trios to take turns shouting out the effects they listed on the last portion of their handout. As teenagers mention their ideas, use the dry-erase marker to write a short summary of each idea directly on the mirror. Strategically space out what you write so that the entire mirror will be covered with the effects of sin once all the teenagers have finished sharing. (If you are using several mirrors because of your group size, invite volunteers to help you by writing the same phrases and words on the other mirrors.) Invite teenagers to keep sharing ideas until each trio has shared at least three of the ideas they listed.

As trios shout out their ideas, rephrase them as you write them on the mirror, in order to make them more general. For example, if someone suggests "Adam and Eve were ashamed because they were naked," you could write "shame" or "self-consciousness." Or if a student says "God kicked them out of the Garden of Eden," you could write "separation from God."

Say: Great job diving deeper into this passage. Things haven't changed much since that very first sin! Sin always results in guilt and shame. Let's look at another situation in which someone experienced serious shame.

THE POINT

Invite a volunteer to read John 8:1-5 aloud.

Say: It's pretty likely that none of you have been caught in the act of adultery, but you've probably been caught sinning in other ways. Think for a moment of a situation you've faced in which you've been caught in a sin.

Ask: • Can you relate to this woman? How do you think she felt?

• Up to this point in the story, how do you think her actions have affected her life?

As students share their thoughts, add their answers to the list on the mirror using the dry-erase marker.

Say: Though the circumstances may be different, we're all in the same situation as Adam, Eve, and the woman caught in adultery. We've all felt the effects of shame and guilt in our lives.

LIFE APPLICATION

15 to 20 minutes

A LOOK IN THE MIRROR

Invite teenagers to form a line and step forward one at a time to look at themselves in the mirror. Encourage them to silently read some of the words and phrases written there and to consider what it feels like to see the effects of sin "written across" their bodies. Prompt them to pick out at least one word or phrase that they can relate to—one way sin has affected their own lives. (If you're using multiple mirrors, have teenagers split into smaller groups around the various mirrors.)

After all the teenagers have had a chance to look in the mirror, invite a volunteer to read aloud Romans 3:23.

Say: **This verse says what we all know in our hearts to be true. We have all sinned. Just like the characters in the Bible stories we've read today, our sin has affected our relationship with God.**

But the good news is, there's more to the story! Let's see how Jesus responded to the woman who was about to be stoned.

Invite another student to read aloud John 8:6-11.

Ask:
- Imagine you were the woman in the story. What would you have felt and thought as you saw Jesus' reaction to the situation?
- Did Jesus just overlook the woman's sin? Explain.

Say: Sin results in guilt and shame. **But Jesus had something more planned for this woman. He had great hope for her life! Jesus has the same hope for us. He wants to free us from the sin that causes shame and guilt and hurts our relationship with God.** ⟨THE POINT

Invite teenagers to participate in a prayer activity to wrap up your study, and let them know that they should keep their eyes *open* during the prayer! Hold out a rag and explain that, one at a time, teenagers will have a chance to come forward and erase a word or phrase from the mirror. As they do so, they should pray a simple prayer aloud, saying, "Thank you, Jesus, that you can set us free from..." and then naming the effect of sin they are erasing.

Continue on with this prayer until all the effects of sin have been erased. (If all the words have been erased before all the students have prayed, encourage the final students to say their own personal prayers of thanksgiving aloud.)

Close the prayer by saying:

FYI

Quietly play a favorite CD during this activity to help set the mood for prayer.

STUDY 1 · SHAME ON YOU   13

God, as we look at this mirror, we see what you desire for us. You want us to live lives that aren't branded by shame, guilt, and the other effects of sin. You want us to have a restored relationship with you. Thank you for offering hope to us instead of condemning us. In Jesus' name, amen.

Pique students' interest by letting them know that over the next several studies, the group will be taking a closer look at how Jesus can set people free from sin, guilt, and shame.

I CAN'T BELIEVE I'M DOING THIS!

Loudly sing your favorite song, but sing it opera-style. 	Loudly sing your favorite song, but sing it opera-style. 
 Use your finger to give yourself a pig nose and walk around snorting and saying "oink!"	 Use your finger to give yourself a pig nose and walk around snorting and saying "oink!"
Crawl around on your hands and knees, mooing like a cow. 	Crawl around on your hands and knees, mooing like a cow. 
 Flap your arms (like wings), shake your head, and loudly crow like a rooster.	 Flap your arms (like wings), shake your head, and loudly crow like a rooster.
Do your best impersonation of an infant: suck your thumb and cry like crazy! 	Do your best impersonation of an infant: suck your thumb and cry like crazy! 

Permission to photocopy this handout from Faith 4 Life: Senior High Bible Study Series, *Believing in Jesus* granted for local church use. Copyright © Group Publishing, Inc., P.O. Box 481, Loveland, CO 80539. www.grouppublishing.com

Read GENESIS 3:1-24 with your partner, and discuss the following questions:

- How do you think Adam and Eve felt after they ate the fruit? NOTES:

- What evidence from the passage suggests what they may have been feeling? NOTES:

- How did their sin affect them? Look specifically at how it affected their view of themselves, their relationship with each other, their relationship with God, or any other effects you can find. List at least five effects.

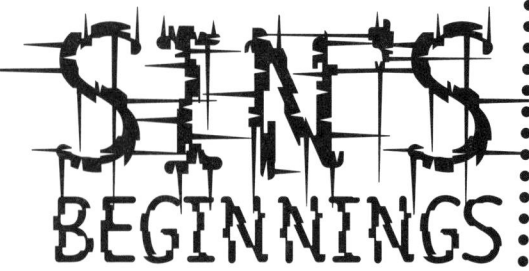

STUDY 2

I WAS WRONG

"I didn't do it!"
"I get blamed for everything!"
"I didn't do anything wrong!"
"It's not my fault!"

Admitting that we've done something wrong doesn't come easily. In fact, admitting that we're wrong is so painful that most of the time we use these (and other) defenses to try to prove our innocence.

The easiest defense is simply to deny any involvement: "You're accusing the wrong person. Someone else did it!" This approach is especially effective, or so it seems, when we follow it up with the standard appeal for pity: "You blame me for everything—even when I haven't done anything wrong!"

Of course, if we've been caught red-handed, we take a different tack. We argue that our actions have been misunderstood, that there was nothing wrong with what we did. Or perhaps we attempt to shift the blame to someone else: a sibling, an enemy, or society at large. The game of avoiding blame goes on and on and on.

Common as they are, these defenses simply don't work with God. God knows when we've done something wrong, and the only words he wants to hear from us are "I was wrong." God wants all of us, teenagers and adults, to admit our sins and honestly confess when we've done something wrong, because that's the only way we'll ever be able to change our ways and experience forgiveness.

This study will help your teenagers learn what repentance is all about and why it is so vital to spiritual and personal growth. This knowledge will enable your teenagers not only to face their own shortcomings, but also to overcome the sins with which they so often struggle.

THE POINT

To overcome sin, we must admit we're wrong.

SCRIPTURE SOURCE

1 Samuel 13:2-14
Samuel announces that God will punish Saul for offering a sinful sacrifice and blaming his sin on others.

Psalm 51:1-17
David confesses his sin, commits to change his ways, and asks God to help him keep his commitment.

Jonah 3:1-10
Jonah warns of God's judgment, so the Ninevites repent of their evil ways.

THE STUDY AT A GLANCE

#1 For Starters
10-15 Minutes

■ BEATING THE RAP

What students will do:
Try to defend themselves against a "crime" they committed, and tie themselves together if they're found guilty.

SUPPLIES:
- "Facts of the Case" handouts (p. 26)
- pencils
- paper
- strips of ribbon or narrow cloth

#2 Bible Truth
25-35 Minutes

■ THE KEY TO FREEDOM

What students will do:
Cover a sheet of newsprint with sins common to teenagers, then creatively teach one another about negative and positive examples of repentance in the Bible.

SUPPLIES:
- Bibles
- paper
- pencils
- newsprint
- tape
- markers
- index cards
- copies of the "Biblical Repentance" handout (p. 27)

#3 Life Application
up to 10 Minutes

■ BREAKING THE BONDS

What students will do:
Apply what they've learned by silently confessing their sins and then cutting themselves free from group members.

SUPPLIES:
- Bible
- index cards from "The Key to Freedom" activity
- markers or pencils
- several pairs of scissors

■ BONUS ACTIVITY
up to 5 Minutes

What students will do:
Reflect on the passages they've studied and use their pieces of cloth as bookmarks in their Bibles.

SUPPLIES:
- strips of ribbon or narrow cloth from "Beating the Rap" activity

BEFORE THE STUDY

Before the study, take some time to prepare the supplies you'll need for each activity. For "Beating the Rap," photocopy the "Facts of the Case" handout (p. 26). You'll need one copy for every four students. Cut narrow strips of ribbon or cloth, about 18 to 24 inches in length, one strip for every student.

For "The Key to Freedom," make one photocopy of the "Biblical Repentance" handout (p. 27) for every eight students. Then cut apart the two sections of the handout. You'll need one section for every four students. Also write the following questions on a sheet of newsprint and hang it where everyone can see it:

- What sins were mentioned in your Scripture?
- How did the person(s) sinning react to the sin?
- How did God respond to the person(s) sinning?

FOR STARTERS

10 to 15 minutes

BEATING THE RAP

Have teenagers form "defense teams" of four teenagers each. Give each defense team a copy of the "Facts of the Case" handout (p. 26) and a pencil. Then tell teenagers they have five minutes to prepare their defense against the charges and evidence described on the handout. Although they actually committed this crime, they are to devise any strategy they can to refute, call into question, or explain away the evidence. Each team will have one minute to present its defense.

Allow teams five minutes to think up their defenses, then ask team representatives to present their teams' defenses. While each representative is talking, listen carefully and jot down notes on a sheet of paper.

When all the teams have presented their defenses, announce a verdict for each team. If any groups simply admitted they were wrong, promised not to commit the crime again, and threw themselves on the mercy of the court, declare those groups guilty but promise to help them change their ways. Declare all other teams guilty, explaining that they didn't present acceptable defenses. Give team members each a ribbon or a strip of narrow cloth, and

To prevent injuries, make sure teenagers don't tie themselves together too tightly. In addition, be sure you have several pairs of scissors handy in case teenagers need to evacuate the room or the building in a hurry.

instruct them to tie their ankles or wrists together with the cloth. Announce that each team will remain tied together until the end of the study.

Then have team members discuss the following questions. After each question, ask volunteers to report their teams' answers.

Ask:
- What was the easiest part of preparing your defense? What was the hardest?
- What are some ways we defend ourselves when we're wrong in real life?
- What did you like about defending yourself when you knew you were wrong?
- How is this like the way you react to sin in real life? How is it different?
- How does defending yourself when you're wrong "tie you up" in real life?

Then **say:**

Your dream defense teams may have beaten the rap in a real court of law, but you're dreaming if you believe you can fool God into thinking you're innocent when you're not. In fact, there's only one way for us to avoid being tied up by sin and its consequences. So today we're going to discuss how we must admit we're wrong in order to overcome sin.

BIBLE TRUTH

25 to 35 minutes

THE KEY TO FREEDOM

Keep teenagers in their groups of four. Give each group a sheet of paper and a pencil. Then challenge groups to list all the sins they can that teenagers struggle with. Explain that groups have two minutes to fill their sheets with sins.

While groups are working, hang a sheet of newsprint. After two minutes, have groups take turns reporting one sin at a time. Write each sin on the newsprint. Continue until every group has reported all the sins it listed. If you haven't covered the newsprint with sins, challenge teenagers to call out additional sins until the entire newsprint is covered with sins.

Then **ask** the entire group the following questions:

- How difficult was it to think of sins that teenagers struggle with?
- How might the list change if we listed sins this group struggles with?
- What does this imply about how widespread sin is? how powerful it is?
- Why do you think teenagers struggle with so many different sins?

Give each person an index card and a pencil. Instruct each person to think of the one sin he or she struggles with most. It can be a sin listed on the newsprint or some other sin the person didn't want to mention earlier.

Allow a minute of thinking time, then have each student draw a symbol to represent that sin on his or her index card. (If you have markers available, let teenagers use them to draw their symbols.) When teenagers finish their cards, direct them to fold them in half so the symbols are hidden, but to keep their cards for use later in the study.

When everyone has finished his or her card, have teenagers discuss the following questions in their small groups.

Ask:
- How difficult was it to admit that you struggle with that sin?
- How do you feel about yourself whenever you commit that sin?
- How do you think God feels about you whenever you commit it?

STUDY 2 · I WAS WRONG 21

- How does it affect your relationship with God?
- Why is it so hard for you to stop doing what you know is wrong?
- How would your life be better if you could overcome that sin?

Then **say**:

> Sin is one of the strongest forces known to humanity. In fact, sin sometimes gets such a grip on our lives that, even when we know what we're doing is wrong, we're powerless to stop it. But God is stronger than any sin, and he wants to help free us from our sins and restore our relationship with him. To overcome sin, we must admit we're wrong. So let's discover what God's Word says about how admitting we're wrong helps us experience God's forgiveness—and empowers us to change our ways.

Assign half the groups 1 Samuel 13:2-14 and the other half Jonah 3:1-10. Give groups copies of the appropriate sections of the "Biblical Repentance" handout (p. 27). Then direct groups to read their passages and sections of the handout.

When groups finish reading, tell them they have three minutes to answer the questions on the newsprint you've posted on the wall. Give each group a pencil, and encourage groups to record their answers on the back of their handouts, because they'll be teaching the rest of the group what they learn.

After three minutes, challenge each group to think up a creative way to teach the other groups what they learned from their passages. For example, groups might act out the events in a play or silly opera, turn the story into a poem or a series of cartoons, or create a newscast describing what happened. Tell groups they have five minutes to think up and create their lessons.

When time is up, have groups take turns presenting their lessons to everyone else. Encourage teenagers to applaud each effort. Once every group has presented, have teenagers **discuss** the following questions in their small groups:

- Which was worse: Saul's sin or the Ninevites' sins? Explain.
- What do you think God should have done to Saul? to the Ninevites?
- Why do you think God punished Saul? Why did he forgive the Ninevites?
- What do these passages teach about how God feels about sin?

> ***FYI**
>
> If teenagers aren't familiar with the story of David and Bathsheba, briefly recap it for them (2 Samuel 11–12). Be sure to mention that David committed adultery with Bathsheba and then had her husband killed so he could take Bathsheba as his wife. This displeased God greatly, so God sent the prophet Nathan to confront David with his sin. When Nathan pointed out David's guilt, David repented with the simple and sincere confession, "I have sinned against the Lord."

FYI

If teenagers need help understanding the important elements of repentance, share these principles with them:

- Repentance means admitting we're wrong. We must not only recognize that what we have done is sinful in God's eyes but also feel sorry for what we've done. When we view our sinful actions from God's holy perspective, we'll feel sad and remorseful about our sins. This, in turn, will lead us to confess our sins to God and to ask God to forgive them. (See Psalm 51:1-2, 3-5, 6-9.)

- Repentance means committing to change our ways. We must decide that we will do whatever we can to keep from committing the same sin over and over again. (See Psalm 51:13-15; Jonah 3:8, 10.)

- Repentance means asking God to help us keep our commitment. None of us has the ability to defeat sin on our own. We need to ask God to give us the power and the perseverance to truly turn from our sins and to develop an obedient character that honors and pleases him. (See Psalm 51:10-15.)

● **What do they reveal about what God is most concerned with?**

When groups finish their discussions, ask volunteers to report the groups' answers to each question. Then **say:**

> **God is more concerned with our response to sin than with the "size" of the sins we commit. All sin is unacceptable to God, so he wants to help us break its hold on our lives. God wants us to repent of our sins. So let's spend a few moments analyzing Psalm 51, David's prayer of repentance after his sin with Bathsheba.**

Tell group members they are to read Psalm 51:1-17 together to identify the different components of true repentance. Assign each group one of the following elements:
- what David said about his sin
- what David committed to do
- what David asked God to do

Give each group some paper to take notes on so they can report back to the entire group. Allow groups several minutes to work, then have them explain what they discovered. When all the groups have reported, **ask** the entire class the following questions:

● **What do you think are the basic elements of repentance?**

● **Which of these elements is the most difficult to do? Why?**

● **What will God do for people who genuinely repent of a sin?**

● **What do you think will happen if someone refuses to repent?**

Then **say:**

> **Psalm 51 shows us that true repentance requires much more than simply saying we're sorry. Genuine repentance involves admitting that we're wrong, committing to change our ways, and asking Jesus to forgive us. To overcome sin and have a close relationship with God, we must admit we're wrong.** ◀ **THE POINT**

Life Application

up to 10 minutes

BREAKING THE BONDS

Have teenagers take out their index cards from the Bible Truth section. Instruct students to look at the symbols and then **discuss** the following questions in their small groups:

- How do you think God feels about your sin? about you?
- What do you think God wants you to do about this sin?
- Without revealing what sin you're referring to, what makes it hard for you to stop committing this sin?
- What will happen if you repent of it? if you don't repent?
- How will admitting you're wrong affect your relationship with God?

After groups finish answering the questions, ask volunteers to report their groups' responses. Then give each group a marker or a pencil. Tell teenagers that you'd like them to draw the "No" sign (a circle with a slash through it) over the symbols of their sin while you read from Psalm 51.

Read Psalm 51:1-12, then ask teenagers to spend one minute in silent prayer, confessing their sins to God, asking for Jesus' forgiveness, and committing themselves to change their ways. After one minute, have group members take turns cutting the ribbons or cloth strips tying them together. Instruct each student to say, "I've admitted my sin, and I've asked Jesus for forgiveness" when they cut themselves free.

Say: We can seek Jesus' forgiveness because he loves us unconditionally. In fact, he loves us so much that he willingly died on a cross to pay the penalty for our sins. Next week we're going to take a closer look at what Jesus did for us on the cross.

When everyone has cut the ribbon, have group members conclude by each praying aloud for the person on the right, thanking God for that person's commitment to repent of his or her sin and to live in a way that pleases God.

Encourage teenagers to each take home a strip of ribbon as a reminder of the importance of freeing themselves of sin, and that admitting they're wrong is the first step in changing their ways and experiencing forgiveness.

To add extra impact to the upcoming study on Jesus' death (Study 3), collect the index cards and set them aside for use in Study 3's Life Application activity, "Hammer and Nail."

BONUS ACTIVITY
up to 5 minutes

If you have time, invite teenagers to spend a moment thinking about the Bible passages they've read or learned about during the study. Take a moment to verbally summarize each of the passages, and then encourage teenagers to decide which passage or verse means the most to them. Invite them to turn to a partner and explain what they chose and why. Prompt students to each use their piece of ribbon as a bookmark in their Bible, marking the passage they selected as a symbol of their commitment to repent of their sins.

FACTS OF THE CASE

You are on trial for a crime you actually committed. Your task is to devise a defense that will convince the judge that you are innocent (or at least that you shouldn't be punished). Read the "facts of the case" below, then work with your group to think up your defense.

The Accused

You're a good student and president of the junior class. You carry a B average in school, and you're active in your church youth group. You live with your mother, father, and two younger sisters. Your parents manage a local restaurant together, and they also lead a church Bible study in their spare time.

The Charges

You're on trial for vandalizing your high school biology teacher's car.

The Evidence

One week prior to the incident, your parents were notified that you were in danger of failing biology. When your parents confronted you with the notice, you lost your temper and claimed that your teacher was "out to get you."

The school janitor claims to have seen you in the vicinity of the car thirty minutes before the damage was discovered.

The car appears to have been struck repeatedly with a tire iron, and your tire iron bears traces of paint that match the color of the car.

Permission to photocopy this handout from Faith 4 Life: Senior High Bible Study Series, *Believing in Jesus* granted for local church use. Copyright © Group Publishing, Inc., P.O. Box 481, Loveland, CO 80539. www.grouppublishing.com

BIBLICAL REPENTANCE

SAUL

Some time prior to the incident recorded in this story, God had told the prophet Samuel to designate Saul as Israel's first king (1 Samuel 9:1–10:3). To prove that Saul was his choice for king, God had even given Saul the ability to prophesy (1 Samuel 10:4-13) and victory over Israel's enemies (1 Samuel 11:1-11). Because Saul had been chosen specifically by God to lead and rule the people, he was obligated to obey God in all that he did (1 Samuel 10:25).

Unfortunately, Saul feared the Israelites more than he feared God. He hid in the baggage when Samuel tried to present him as king (1 Samuel 10:20-23), and he blamed other people for his own poor decisions on several occasions (1 Samuel 13:11-12; 14:43-45; 15:20-21, 24, 30). As a result of Saul's weak disobedience, God eventually replaced him with David, a man after God's own heart.

THE NINEVITES

During Jonah's lifetime, Nineveh was the capital of the ancient empire of Assyria, Israel's most hated and feared enemy. Therefore, it isn't surprising that Jonah initially resisted (and even fled) God's command to go to Nineveh and to warn of impending judgment (Jonah 1:1-3). Jonah was afraid that the hated Ninevites would not believe his prophetic warning and repent of their sins (Jonah 4:1-2). Jonah may have also feared what the Ninevites would do to him—a prophet of Israel—for telling them that they were sinfully wrong.

But God was determined that the Ninevites hear the warning, so he saved Jonah from a watery death (Jonah 1:11–2:10) and then sent him to deliver his prophetic message to the Ninevites. When Jonah finally warned the Ninevites of God's coming judgment, the citizens and the king of the city proclaimed a fast—no food or drink—and wore dark, rough cloth instead of their regular clothes. By adopting these ancient mourning practices, the Ninevites intended to demonstrate the genuineness of their prayers of confession and contrition.

Permission to photocopy this handout from Faith 4 Life: Senior High Bible Study Series, *Believing in Jesus* granted for local church use. Copyright © Group Publishing, Inc., P.O. Box 481, Loveland, CO 80539. www.grouppublishing.com

STUDY 3

SENTENCED TO DEATH

John 3:16 is a pretty "popular" verse. Banners bearing the Scripture reference are almost always displayed somewhere in the crowd at professional sporting events. Preschool Sunday school classes work *hard* to memorize it (even though they may not quite understand what it means to *perish*). It's pretty familiar, and so is the story the verse refers to. Teenagers have heard about Jesus' death before. The cross is probably the most recognized symbol of Christianity.

So learning about Jesus' death is bound to be pretty boring. Blah, blah, blah.

Not exactly.

This study will open teenagers' eyes, ears, and hearts as they step inside the event that changed the world. They'll be challenged as they consider what Jesus really went through, and they'll be convicted when they realize the reason he did it: *his love for them*.

Through this exploration of the crucifixion, teenagers will be presented with the awesome truth that they can receive forgiveness for their sins through faith in Christ, and they'll have an opportunity to respond to God in worship and prayer.

THE POINT

Through Jesus' death on the cross, we can receive forgiveness for our sins.

SCRIPTURE SOURCE

Psalm 22
This psalm includes prophecies of the suffering Jesus would endure on the cross.

Matthew 27:32-56
Matthew describes Jesus' crucifixion.

John 3:16
This verse explains that people who believe in Jesus can have eternal life.

THE STUDY AT A GLANCE

#1 For Starters
10-15 Minutes

■ THE PAIN

What students will do:
Experience how God sees sin.

SUPPLIES:
- "My Life" handouts (p. 36)
- pencils
- tape
- markers

■ BONUS ACTIVITY
up to 10 Minutes

What students will do:
Build a wall and discover what divides people and God.

SUPPLIES:
- 20 or more cardboard boxes
- newsprint
- tape
- markers

#2 Bible Truth
20-25 Minutes

■ AND YOU WERE THERE

What students will do:
Examine the Crucifixion from a "first-person" perspective.

SUPPLIES:
- Bibles
- 5 candles in candleholders
- matches
- "At the Cross" handouts (p. 37)

#3 Life Application
15-20 Minutes

■ HAMMER AND NAIL

What students will do:
Nail their sins to a cross and consider how Jesus' death impacts their own lives.

SUPPLIES:
- Bibles
- 2 pieces of wood
- hammer
- nails
- pencils
- "My Life" handouts from "The Pain" activity
- tape

BEFORE THE STUDY

Before the study, make one photocopy of the "My Life" handout (p. 36) for every student, and gather enough markers so each participant can use one.

If you choose to do the Bonus Activity, you'll also need to gather at least twenty cardboard boxes. A variety of shapes and sizes will work best.

For the Bible Truth section, make enough photocopies of "At the Cross" handout (p. 37) so that each student can have one. You'll also need five candles in candleholders and some matches.

For "Hammer and Nail," you'll need to create a simple wooden cross. You'll need two pieces of wood for this activity—2x4s work best. Cut the wood so that one board is 5 feet long and the other is 3 feet long. Use a few nails to create a makeshift cross, and gather enough nails so that each participant can use one.

FOR STARTERS

10 to 15 minutes

THE PAIN

Give teenagers each a "My Life" handout (p. 36) and a pencil, and have them complete the handouts. Afterward, have students tape their handouts to the wall. Give everyone a marker.

Say: These papers represent who you are. For this next activity, we'll imagine these papers *are* you.

On "go," use the markers to deface your own handout. You may write derogatory names on the sheets, but don't use profanity. You can scribble on your faces. You may even tear the papers if you want. When I call time, stop defacing the papers and step back from the wall.

Give teenagers a minute or two to deface the handouts. Then have teenagers collect their papers and sit in a circle.

Ask:
- How do you feel as you look at your paper?
- How is that like the way God feels when he sees our sins?
- How did you feel as you defaced your paper?
- In what ways do we sometimes deface Jesus?

*FYI

This study includes activities that are meant to tap into teenagers' emotions, so be prepared for their responses to the lesson. Some may giggle or laugh because they feel uncomfortable and don't know how else to release tension. Others may cry during the activities. Be flexible during the discussion times, allowing time for teenagers to respond to God from their hearts. Also, be sure to encourage all the participants to respect one another's feelings.

notes

- Who were the people who "defaced" Jesus at the time of his crucifixion?
- Look at your paper. How does the way it looks reflect what sin does to our lives?

Say: Just as we may have felt bad about the ruined papers, God is deeply saddened by the effects of sin in our lives. He wanted to reconcile the world to himself, so he sent Jesus to die for our sins and take the punishment we deserve. Though *we* deserved to die, Jesus died in our place. Jesus' agony on the cross was much more than physical pain. He shouldered the sins of the world as he hung from the cross.

Through Jesus' death on the cross, we can receive forgiveness for our sins.

⟩⟩ BONUS ACTIVITY

up to 10 minutes

If you have time, try this activity before or after "The Pain."

Place the boxes, newsprint, and tape in the center of the room. Have students form two groups and have each stay on one side of an imaginary line in the middle of the room.

Say: Take the next few minutes to build a wall down the center of the room. Make it as tall and wide as you can, using these supplies. You may work together on the wall, but you may not communicate with the people on the other side of the wall. You must stay on your side of the "line" where the wall will be built.

After a few minutes, call time. Give each student a marker. Have them each write on their side of the wall things that build walls between them and God such as lying, bad language, or deception.

Then have groups switch sides and read the other group's wall.

Ask: ● How did you feel as you were building the wall?

● How is building this wall like building walls between you and God?

Say: Our sins create walls that separate us from God, but Jesus willingly died on the cross in order to break down those walls. Today we'll explore Jesus' crucifixion and see what it means for each of us.

Have teenagers break down the wall.

20 to 25 minutes

AND YOU WERE THERE

Place five candles in a circle. Light them and turn out the lights. Give teenagers each an "At the Cross" handout (p. 37).

Say: Imagine what it was like. Even thought it was daytime, it was dark. Imagine what the people felt as Jesus died. This handout contains a short script based on Jesus' crucifixion. Follow the instructions and read together when your part comes up.

Read the narrator's part, and have teenagers follow along and read the guys' or girls' parts as appropriate. Teenagers will have to stay close to the candles to read their scripts. As the script is read, blow out one candle every time you see a small candle icon on the script. Just after teenagers read the last section, blow out the final candle, and remain silent for a moment.

Turn on the lights, and invite teenagers to form pairs and **discuss** the following questions:

- How did you feel as you read the script?
- What stood out to you most from the reading? Why?
- What was the hardest part to read or listen to? Why?
- Imagine you were there when Jesus was crucified. How do you think you would have reacted?

Invite teenagers to gather back together in a large group, and **say:**

Let's take a closer look at what really happened when Jesus died on the cross. As you listen to the story, imagine yourself in the crowd, observing all that took place.

Invite a volunteer to read aloud Matthew 27:32-56 while the rest of the students read along in their Bibles.

Ask:
- What does this Scripture passage tell us about Jesus' death on the cross?
- What do you think the physical pain Jesus suffered might have been like?
- Do you think Jesus also suffered emotional or spiritual pain? Explain.
- In his life, Jesus performed many miracles, including raising people from the dead. Why didn't Jesus perform a miracle to save himself from being crucified?
- What does Jesus' death have to do with your life?

Say: The Bible tells us that Jesus died on the cross so we could receive forgiveness for our sins and so our relationship with God could be restored. Let's take some time to consider how Jesus' death impacts our lives today.

LIFE APPLICATION

15 to 20 minutes

HAMMER AND NAIL

Silently nail the two pieces of wood together to form a cross. Dim the lights.

Say: When Jesus died on the cross, he paid the price for our sins. I'm going to give each of you a pencil. On the back of your "My Life" handout, write key words to describe areas in your life where you need God's forgiveness. You don't need to describe these areas specifically, just use a word or two to remind you. In a few minutes, we'll nail these papers to a wooden cross. Work silently, and then come up one at a time when you're ready. While others are coming up to the cross, use the time for personal reflection and prayer. Listen to the hammering and think about Jesus' sacrifice for you.

Distribute pencils to teenagers. (Some people might also need tape to put their handouts back together.) After you've completed your handout, go up to the cross and use a nail to attach it to the cross. Help direct teenagers who come up after you.

When everyone has nailed his or her paper to the cross, invite teenagers to sit in a circle and read aloud John 3:16. Use the verse to affirm each teenager's importance to God. Go around the circle and have teenagers join you in repeating the verse, using each person's name in place of "the world." For example, as you come to Micah, you'd say, "For God so loved Micah that he gave his one and only Son, that whoever believes in him shall not perish but have eternal life."

When you've finished, **say:**

Through Jesus' death on the cross, we can receive forgiveness for our sins. **Just as this verse says, God loves each of us deeply. It is through faith in Jesus that our relationship with God can be restored and we can have eternal life in heaven with God.**

Jesus' death on the cross was a powerful event. The whole world shuddered with his death. Yet by his death on the cross, we've all been given life. Our sins died on the cross with Jesus.

Spend a moment or two in prayer around the cross. Thank God for sacrificing his Son for you. Take some time to silently ask God for forgiveness for your sins.

Instead of having teenagers write sins on their handouts, pass out the index cards you may have collected from the Study 2 activity, "Breaking the Bonds." Have teenagers nail their cards instead of their handouts to the cross.

If you have students with zero carpentry experience or some whom you just don't trust with a hammer, station yourself near the cross so that you can show each student how to safely hammer his or her nail. If necessary, you could also offer to hammer the nails for some students who don't feel comfortable doing so themselves.

If you have a large group and it would take a long time to repeat John 3:16 for each student, have teenagers form pairs and read the verse aloud to each other, again replacing "the world" with their partner's name.

After teenagers leave, collect the handouts or cards they nailed to the cross by tearing them off. Keep all the nails stuck in the cross (if any come loose, hammer them back in). Discard the handouts or cards. Hide the cross somewhere and save it for Study 4.

If you still aren't sure what you think of Jesus, simply think about what you've heard today, or ask God to help you understand the importance of Jesus' death for your life.

After a few minutes, invite teenagers to form a tight circle around the cross, pick up the cross, and quietly carry it to a closet or a corner of the room that represents a tomb. Have volunteers close in prayer.

MY LIFE

Think of this handout as a picture of you. Complete the sections below to describe your life.

NAME _____

{ THREE UNIQUE THINGS ABOUT ME ARE . . .

{ IF I COULD DO ANYTHING I WANTED, I'D . . .

{ IF I WERE TO DESCRIBE MYSELF TO A STRANGER, I'D SAY . . .

DRAW A SELF-PORTRAIT BELOW.

{ MY LIFE IS . . .

AT THE CROSS

There are three different parts in this drama: Narrator, Guys, and Girls. Read aloud your part in turn. (This script is based upon Matthew 27:32-56. The reading is from Psalm 22:1, 6-7, 14a, 15a, 16b, 17-18.)

Narrator: At noon, the whole country was covered with darkness. The people watched as Jesus hung on the cross. Some were there out of curiosity. Some came to cry for him. Others came to mock him. Out of the darkness, Jesus cried aloud from the cross, "My God, my God, why have you forsaken me?"

Guys: What did he say?

Girls: He's crying out for his God.

Narrator: People nearby tried to make Jesus drink some cheap wine. They took a sponge, soaked it in the wine, and held it out on a long stick to Jesus' lips.

Guys: Here, drink it. Drink it! It'll ease the pain.

Girls: Wait, let him suffer! Let's see if Elijah is coming to save him now.

Narrator: *(A loud cry of Jesus' dying breath)* "Ahhhhhh!" *(Pause)* With one final cry, Jesus gave up his spirit. Suddenly the earth shook. Graves opened, and people who were buried came to life. Everywhere, people scattered in panic.

Girls: What's that? What's happening?

Guys: *(Frightened)* It's an earthquake! Run!

Girls: What does this mean?

Guys: It's him! It's all because of Jesus.

Girls: It can't be. He's just a man...or could he be...?

Guys: The Son of God?

All: He was the Son of God. Oh, how I wish I'd followed him.

Narrator: A reading from Psalm 22, the psalm Jesus quoted from when he said, "My God, my God, why have you forsaken me?"

Girls: My God, my God, why have you forsaken me? Why are you so far from saving me, so far from the words of my groaning?

Guys: I am a worm and not a man, scorned by men and despised by the people. All who see me mock me; they hurl insults, shaking their heads.

Girls: I am poured out like water, and all my bones are out of joint. My strength is dried up and my tongue sticks to the roof of my mouth.

Guys: A band of evil men has encircled me, they have pierced my hands and my feet. I can count all my bones; people stare and gloat over me.

Girls: They divide my garments among them and cast lots for my clothing.

Permission to photocopy this handout from Faith 4 Life: Senior High Bible Study Series, *Believing in Jesus* granted for local church use. Copyright © Group Publishing, Inc., P.O. Box 481, Loveland, CO 80539. www.grouppublishing.com

STUDY 4

HE IS RISEN INDEED!

T.G.F.S!

Friday was the worst. It was the day Jesus was tortured, beaten, and publicly executed. It was the day Jesus breathed his last. His lifeless body was placed in a tomb. It was a dark, dark, day.

Then came Saturday. The disciples were in hiding, fearing for their lives. Those who'd followed Jesus were confused, discouraged, completely shocked. It was the Sabbath, but for those who loved Jesus, it was not a day of refreshing rest. Could it really all be over?

Thank God for Sunday! Early that morning, Mary Magdalene and some other followers of Jesus were the first to hear the news: Jesus was alive! And then they saw him! They fell at his feet and worshipped him. Soon the other disciples would see him too—and their lives would be forever changed.

This study will challenge teenagers about their own response to the Resurrection. Will they deny that Jesus really rose from the dead? Or will they respond in faith, worship, and commitment?

THE POINT
Through faith in Jesus, we can experience new life.

SCRIPTURE SOURCE

Matthew 28:1-15
Matthew describes Jesus' resurrection from the dead.

Matthew 28:16-20
Jesus commissions his followers to make disciples of all nations.

Romans 10:9-11
The writer explains that faith in Jesus provides salvation.

THE STUDY AT A GLANCE

#1 For Starters
up to 15 Minutes

■ **SURPRISE!**

What students will do:
Experience being surprised and talk about resurrection joy.

SUPPLIES:
- balloons
- streamers
- confetti
- the wooden cross from Study 3
- candle
- matches
- snacks

#2 Bible Truth
20-30 Minutes

■ **ROLLING THE STONE AWAY**

What students will do:
Discuss Mary's joy and turn rocks into symbols of the Resurrection.

SUPPLIES:
- Bibles
- several medium-sized rocks
- paint
- paintbrushes
- paper

#3 Life Application
10-15 Minutes

■ **JOY YEAR-ROUND**

What students will do:
Brainstorm practical ways to live with resurrection joy every day.

SUPPLIES:
- Bibles
- "Joy Surprise" handouts (p. 46)
- pencils
- tape
- hammer

■ **BONUS ACTIVITY**
up to 10 Minutes

What students will do:
Affirm one another by trading balloons.

SUPPLIES:
- balloons from "Surprise!"
- permanent marker

BEFORE THE STUDY

Before the study, prepare a room that can easily be darkened for the "Surprise!" activity by decorating it with colorful balloons, streamers, and confetti. (If you choose to do the Bonus Activity, you'll need to make sure you have at least one balloon per student in the room you are decorating.) This room should be different from your regular meeting area. Make the room as colorful as you can. If space is tight at your church, consider using a basement room or kitchen for this activity. Place the cross from Study 3 on the floor near the entrance to the room. (Check that all the papers have been removed from the previous study's activity.) Make sure all the lights are out and the room is very dark—use black plastic to cover windows if necessary. Place lots of yummy snacks on a table in the room. Finally, lock the door so teenagers don't wander into the room by accident.

For the Bible Truth section, you'll need to collect several medium-sized rocks, each about 3 to 6 inches in diameter. You'll need one rock for every group of four students. Set out painting supplies (paints, brushes, paper) on a table in the room. Tempera paint will work best for this activity, though acrylic or oil paints will also work. Gather enough painting supplies so that all of the students can participate.

For the "Joy Year-Round" activity, make enough photocopies of the "Joy Surprise" handout (p. 46) so that each student can have one.

FOR STARTERS

up to 15 minutes

SURPRISE!

Say: During our last study, we experienced the pain of Jesus' death on the cross. Our next activity is serious. We're going to visit Jesus' tomb. As we leave this room, let's quietly reflect on the sacrifice Jesus made on the cross.

Take teenagers silently to the room you prepared. Light a small candle and walk into the entrance of the room (don't let anyone turn on the lights). Place the candle near the cross, and form a circle around the cross.

Say: Jesus' death set us free from sin. Think about how difficult it must have been for Jesus to give his life for others—especially since many of them despised him.

Have teenagers close their eyes to think and pray silently for thirty seconds. Then **say:**

Imagine how Jesus' followers felt. Many had given up *everything* to be with Jesus. But he died! All hope was lost!

Have teenagers close their eyes to think and pray silently for thirty more seconds.

When time is up, blow out the candle, turn on the lights, and yell: **Surprise!**

Say: Jesus has risen from the dead! Let's celebrate!

Have teenagers toss the balloons and streamers around the room in celebration. Encourage teenagers to enjoy the snacks.

While teenagers are munching their snacks, have them form groups of three to five and **discuss** these questions:

- What were you thinking when you first entered this room?
- If you had been one of Jesus' followers, what do you think you might have been feeling after he died and was buried?
- How was the surprise of this celebration like the surprise of Jesus' resurrection?
- What's the greatest surprise that's ever happened to you?
- What emotions do you think Jesus' followers might have experienced when they realized Jesus had risen from the dead?

Say: During our last study, we attached papers to the cross—papers listing sins we needed forgiveness for. Today those papers are gone. As Jesus died on the cross, our sins died with him. By rising again, Jesus also conquered death and provided us a path to God. Through personal faith in Jesus, we can experience new life.

Give teenagers a couple of minutes to continue enjoying the snacks, then have everyone go back to the regular meeting area.

To add more fun to the celebration party, play some upbeat music. Pick songs that your students like, and feel free to turn up the volume!

If you plan on doing the Bonus Activity at the end of the study, have teenagers each collect a balloon to take back with them to the regular meeting room. Have them set the balloons aside until they're needed.

ROLLING THE STONE AWAY

Have students form new groups of four and read Matthew 28:1-15.

Ask: • What are the important events that happened in this passage?

• What emotions do you think the women experienced when the angel spoke to them at the tomb?

• How do you think they reacted when they saw Jesus? How would you have felt?

• What emotions do you think the guards experienced after the incident at the tomb?

• How do you think they felt after they were asked to lie about what happened?

Invite groups to share what they discussed, then **say:**

These two groups of people responded to Jesus' resurrection in totally different ways. The women celebrated in faith and worship, while the guards and chief priests denied the truth. We have a similar choice: We each must decide how we will personally react to Jesus' death and resurrection. Will we respond in faith? Or will we deny that he ever rose from the dead?

Give each group a rock and **say:**

This small stone represents the gigantic stone that was rolled away when Jesus rose from the dead. It also represents the choice we each must make. We can deny Jesus or, by putting our faith in him, we can experience new life and forgiveness for our sins. ⟨THE POINT⟩

Invite teenagers to use paints and brushes to turn their rocks into symbols of joy. Invite them to use colors and pictures to depict what Jesus' resurrection means to them.

When they've finished, have groups set their rocks aside for a few minutes to dry, and gather everyone together in a large group.

Ask: • What does Jesus' resurrection mean to you?

Have a volunteer read Matthew 28:16-20, then **ask:**

• When Jesus appeared to the disciples, he gave them some instructions. How would you paraphrase what he said in your own words?

FYI

Use these rocks as decorations in your youth room, or set them aside to display during the "Changed 4 Life" worship service suggestion (p. 47). Alternatively, you may want to keep the rocks and use them to decorate the church sanctuary or youth room on Easter Sunday.

- How do you think Jesus' resurrection changed their lives?
- What role does faith play in being a disciple of Jesus?
- How does faith in Jesus' resurrection give us new life?

Prompt groups to get their rocks, display them, and explain what they painted. As each group presents its rock, invite group members to answer the question: **How can we live with resurrection joy every day?**

Say: Just like the women who first went to the empty tomb, and the disciples who worshipped Jesus in Galilee, Jesus' resurrection gives us cause for great joy!

Life Application

10 to 15 minutes

JOY YEAR-ROUND

Say: The joy of Jesus' resurrection doesn't have to begin and end each Easter Sunday. Let's brainstorm practical ways to live joyfully each day.

Give each student a "Joy Surprise" handout (p. 46) and a pencil. Have teenagers complete the handouts.

When they've finished, have them gather in their groups of four from the "Rolling the Stone Away" activity. Prompt teenagers to share their ideas in their groups. Then have each group choose one idea to act out in a short one- to two-minute skit for the rest of the class.

After each group has acted out its skit, **say:**

> We can celebrate resurrection joy in many ways, as we've just seen. Let's commit to use these ideas.

Tape the handouts to the wall, and have teenagers walk around and read them. Ask teenagers to choose at least three ideas and pray silently to God, committing to use these ideas in the coming week.

Say: The most important way we can live in resurrection joy is to put our faith in Jesus and live as his disciples. Just like Jesus' resurrection changed the disciples' lives, our lives can also be made new through faith in Jesus.

Invite a volunteer to read aloud Romans 10:9-11. Ask teenagers to define the following terms from the passage: *confess, Lord, saved, justified,* and *trusts*. (If teenagers need guidance, give your own definitions of the words at the end of the discussion.) Then **say:**

> We each must decide how we will respond to Jesus' resurrection. Some of you may be struggling to determine what you really believe about Jesus. You may not believe he really rose from the dead or you may not be willing to call him "Lord" and commit your life to him. Some of you may be struggling with feelings of guilt over sins that you're not quite sure God will really forgive.
>
> Others of you may be at a point when you've realized that you *do* believe in Jesus' death and resurrection, and you want to experience the forgiveness and new life he offers. You may feel ready to make a commitment to him—the type of commitment this verse describes.

Students will grow to trust you more as they observe your efforts to respect their privacy. Whenever teenagers are asked to write down personal answers to questions, it's always a good idea to let them know if what they write will be kept private or if it will be shared with the group. In this specific case, as students work to fill out their "Joy Surprise" handouts, let them know that their answers and ideas will be shown to the others in the group. This will prevent anyone from writing something deeply personal and then feeling betrayed when his or her handout is publicly posted on the wall.

FYI

Some of the students in your group may not be ready to put their faith in Jesus due to doubts or questions. Others may need your guidance in helping them grow and take their first steps of faith. Let teenagers know that you're available to talk with them one-on-one about how they've responded to Jesus' death and resurrection. Encourage them to be open and honest with you about their thoughts and feelings, so you can try to answer their spiritual questions and so you can support them in prayer.

And some of you may already believe in Jesus. You may be committed to living as a disciple and desiring to grow even more in your faith.

As Romans 10:9-11 explains, through faith in Jesus, we can experience new life. **THE POINT** Let's spend a few moments responding to God in our hearts.

Have teenagers take a moment to think about how they want to personally respond to everything they've learned about sin, forgiveness, and Jesus' death and resurrection. Allow teenagers about one minute to think quietly, then invite them to follow you back into the room you prepared for the "Surprise!" activity. Show them how to remove a nail from the cross using the pronged side of the hammer.

Conclude the study by allowing time for each teenager to remove a nail. Tell them each to think of their nail as a symbol of their personal response to Jesus' resurrection. Encourage each student to take this nail home and put it in a special place, to serve as a reminder of what Jesus has done for him or her.

BONUS ACTIVITY
up to 10 minutes

If you have time after "Joy Year-Round," try this affirmation activity.

Have teenagers each pick up a balloon (from the "Surprise!" activity) and then form a circle. Pass a permanent marker around and have teenagers each write their name on their balloon.

Say: We can also celebrate Jesus' resurrection by supporting one another.

Walk into the center of the circle. Describe a positive trait someone in the circle has shown during the past four weeks, then present your balloon to him or her. Have that person go and stand in the center of the circle, describe another person's positive trait, and then give that person his or her balloon. Traits might include patience, concern for others, kindness, and wisdom. Continue until each person has been in the center of the circle and each person is holding someone else's balloon.

Say: Take your balloon home with you and put it in your room. During the coming week, when you look at the balloon, say a prayer for the person whose name is written on it. Pray for that person to experience the joy of Jesus' resurrection every day.

JOY SURPRISE

What can you do to live out the joy of Jesus' resurrection? In each of the boxes below, write at least two specific things you can do to live in celebration of Jesus' death and resurrection. Use the example in the "school" box to get you started.

At school I can live with resurrection joy by...

1. Sharing my love for Jesus with one person in my English class.
2.

At home I can live with resurrection joy by...

At work I can live with resurrection joy by...

With my family I can live with resurrection joy by...

With non-Christians I can live with resurrection joy by...

Permission to photocopy this handout from Faith 4 Life: Senior High Bible Study Series, *Believing in Jesus* granted for local church use. Copyright © Group Publishing, Inc., P.O. Box 481, Loveland, CO 80539. www.grouppublishing.com

CHANGED 4 LIFE

To help teenagers reflect further on what it means to believe in Jesus, plan a special youth worship service, to be held a few weeks after you conclude these studies. Call the event "Celebrating the Savior," and let teenagers know that this will be their chance to prepare something personal as a way of expressing what Jesus means to them. For example, teenagers could

- design and create paintings, banners, or sculptures;
- write a poem or short story;
- select a favorite verse to share;
- bring in a symbolic object from home and explain what it means;
- prepare a short presentation of their own faith story;
- play a musical piece celebrating Jesus;
- create and present a short drama about new life in Christ; or
- bring in a favorite CD and share a song that reminds them of faith in Christ.

Decide with the students if the event should be just for them or if they'd like to invite parents (or the entire church family) to attend. Be in charge of organizing who is doing what and, especially if you have a large group, encourage teenagers to work together on projects.

Look for the Whole Family of Faith4Life Bible Studies!

Coming Soon!

for Senior High
- Christian Character
- Following Jesus
- Worshipping 24/7
- Your Relationships

for Junior High
- Choosing Wisely
- How to Pray
- My Family Life
- Sharing Jesus

for Preteens
- Building Friendships
- Handling Conflict
- Succeeding in School
- What's a Christian?

Senior High Books
- Applying God's Word
- Believing in Jesus
- Family Matters
- Is There Life After High School?
- Prayer
- Sexuality
- Sharing Your Faith
- Your Christian ID

Junior High Books
- Becoming a Christian
- Fighting Temptation
- Finding Your Identity
- Friends
- God's Purpose for Me
- My Life as a Christian
- Understanding the Bible
- Who Is God?

Preteen Books
- Being Responsible
- Getting Along With Others
- God in My Life
- Going Through Tough Times
- How to Make Great Choices
- Peer Pressure
- The Bible and Me
- Why God Made Me

Visit your local Christian bookstore,
or contact Group Publishing, Inc., at 800-447-1070.
www.grouppublishing.com